# TRAINING,

# ROYAL NAVAL DIVISION.

# TRAINING,

# ROYAL NAVAL DIVISION.

---

The increasing demand for drafts necessitates curtailing the time required to train men, and with this object in view the following instructions are issued as a guide.

Eight hours training at least is to be carried out daily except Saturdays (four hours) and Sundays (nil).

W NICHOLLS,
Adjutant-General Royal Marines,
Royal Naval Division.

1915.

# RECRUIT TRAINING, ROYAL NAVAL DIVISION DEPÔT.

## PRINCIPLES.

The five weeks' course contained in the attached Syllabus includes instruction in the following subjects :—

1. Development of the Service spirit.
2. Instructions in Depôt duties, cleanliness, care of feet, smartness, discipline, orders, and such regulations as immediately affect the men of the Royal Naval Division Depôt.
3. Physical training.
4. Squad drill, extended order drill and bayonet fighting.
5. Musketry instruction.
6. Elementary night training.

No recruits are to be detailed for guards or fatigues until they have been passed out of recruit squads by Battalion Commanders.

The squads should, as far as possible, be drilled on the gravel terraces. The grass plots are not suitable for recruit training.

Rifles are to be in the men's possession and not in the battalion armouries.

**Recruit squad instructors are to be permanent throughout the Course,** and an assistant leading seaman should be attached to each squad.

Battalion Officers detailed to supervise the instruction of recruit squads should fulfil the roll of Directors of Instruction, and not act as squad instructors. They should arrange to give lectures to the combined squads and be responsible to their respective Battalion Commanders for the discipline and administration of the squads allotted to them for supervision.

Before being dismissed from this Course every squad will be examined by Battalion Commanders or their representatives, who will determine whether the squad has obtained the necessary standard of efficiency.

a (12)29298 G 976 1500 7/15 E & S 

## 1st Week.

### RECRUIT TRAINING

#### MONDAY.

Kitted up and taken to sleeping quarters and squadded into permanent squads.

#### TUESDAY.

1½ hours.—Lecture by squad instructors.

(*a*) Functions of the Royal Naval Division.

(*b*) Name of Commodore, Staff Officers, Battalion Commanders, Company Officers and Instructors.

(*c*) Rules to observe as regards hygiene, spitting, leave, smoking, washing, bathing, hair-cutting. Hours of parade. Punishments for absence and drunkenness. Methods of making requests and complaints. Compliments paid to officers and ratings. Limits of bounds of the Depôt. Conduct in the sleeping quarters. Conduct outside the Depôt. Duty when ordered to escort. Saluting quarter deck. Reporting sick and bugle calls of the Depôt.

3 hours.—Squads formed in open ranks and taught—

(*a*) Position of attention and dressing with interval.

(*b*) Standing at ease.

(*c*) Saluting by numbers.

1 hour.—Draw rifles, leather gear and cleaning gear.

1 hour.—Parts of rifle.

½ hour.—Catechise squads on lecture given in the morning and demonstrate methods of saluting, making requests and appearing before officers.

1 hour.—Physical training.

#### WEDNESDAY.

2½ hours.—Squad in open ranks.

(*a*) Turnings, judging the time.

(*b*) Length of pace and time in marching.

(*c*) Marking time. Marching in slow time. Turnings on the march.

½ hour.—Lecture on discipline. History of the War and catechism on the previous lecture.

2 hours.—Squad in open ranks.

(a) Changing step, on the march and marking time.
(b) Saluting on the march.
(c) Turnings on the march.

2 hours.—Musketry.
1 hour.—Physical training.

THURSDAY.

2½ hours.—Squad in open ranks.

Repeat all movements of the two previous days in slow time.

½ hour.—Catechism on lectures.
2 hours.—Squad in two ranks.

(a) Marching in line in slow time.
(b) Changing direction in slow time.
(c) Formation of fours.
(d) Marching in fours in slow time.
(e) Diagonal march.

2 hours.—Musketry.
1 hour.—Physical training.

FRIDAY.

4½ hours.—Squads in two ranks.

(a) Marching in line in slow time.
(b) Marching in file and fours.
(c) Forming from file on the march into line (on the left and right form squad).
(d) Wheeling in fours.
(e) Stepping out, stepping short.

2 hours.—Musketry.
½ hour.—Catechism on lectures.
1 hour.—Physical training.

SATURDAY.

2½ hours.—Squad drill in two ranks, in quick time; repeating all the lessons taught during previous four days.
½ hour.—Catechism on previous lectures.
1 hour.—Physical training.

## 2nd Week.

MONDAY.

1 hour.—Lecture on parts of rifle and care of arms.
2 hours.—Rifle exercises, *by numbers only*, order, slope, dismiss

3 hours.—Squad drill with rifles, open ranks, quick time.
1 hour.—Musketry.
1 hour.—Physical training.

TUESDAY.

1 hour.—Rifle exercise by numbers. Present, port arms, trail and ground arms.
3 hours.—Squad drill with rifles, open ranks, quick time.
2 hours.—Squad drill in two ranks.
1 hour.—Musketry.
1 hour.—Physical training.

WEDNESDAY.

2 hours.—Rifle exercises, fixing bayonets, unfixing bayonets, piling arms, shoulder arms, "bv numbers."
2½ hours.—Squad drill in two ranks.
2 hours.—Musketry.
½ hour.—Lecture on hygiene.
1 hour.—Physical training.

THURSDAY.

3 hours.—Squad drill in two ranks.
1 hour.—Care of arms.
2 hours.—Musketry.
1 hour.—Rifle exercises, judging the time.
1 hour.—Physical training.

FRIDAY.

3 hours.—Squad drill in two ranks.
1½ hours.—Bayonet fighting.
1 hour.—Rifle exercises, judging the time.
1 hour.—Physical training.
1½ hours.—Musketry.

SATURDAY.

2½ hours.—Squad drill.
½ hour.—Lecture on hygiene.
1 hour.—Physical training.

## 3rd Week.

MONDAY.

2 hours.—Extended order drill.
2 hours.—Squad drill.

1 hour.—Bayonet fighting.
1 hour.—Physical training.
2 hours.—Musketry.

TUESDAY.

1 hour.—Care of arms.
2 hours.—Squad drill.
1 hour.—Bayonet fighting.
1 hour.—Rifle exercises.
1 hour.—Physical training.
2 hours.—Musketry.

WEDNESDAY.

2 hours.—Extended order drill.
2½ hours.—Squad drill.
½ hour.—Hygiene. Questions to recruits.
1 hour.—Physical training.
2 hours.—Musketry.

THURSDAY.

1 hour.—Bayonet fighting.
1 hour.—Rifle exercises.
2 hours.—Squad drill.
1 hour.—Extended order.
1 hour.—Physical training.
2 hours.—Musketry.

FRIDAY.

2 hours.—Rifle drill.
1 hour.—Extended order.
1 hour.—Rifle exercises.
1 hour.—Slow marching.
1 hour.—Physical training.
2 hours.—Musketry.

SATURDAY.

2 hours.—Squad drill.
1 hour.—Questions on discipline. Hygiene and regulations of the Depôt.
1 hour.—Physical training.

## 4th Week.

### COMMENCEMENT OF ROUTE MARCHING.

MONDAY.

3 hours.—March out to training area, march discipline, and extended order drill.
1 hour.—Squad drill.

1 hour.—Bayonet fighting.
1 hour.—Physical training.
2 hours.—Musketry.

TUESDAY.

2 hours.—Musketry.
2½ hours.—Squad drill.
½ hour.—Lecture on hygiene and discipline.
2 hours.—Firing instruction.
1 hour.—Physical training.

WEDNESDAY.

3 hours.—March out to training area. Firing instruction.
2½ hours.—Squad drill.
1½ hours.—Bayonet fighting.
1 hour.—Physical training.

THURSDAY.

2 hours.—Aiming and firing instruction.
2 hours.—Squad drill.
1 hour.—Bayonet fighting.
1 hour.—Physical training.
2 hours.—Musketry.

FRIDAY.

2½ hours.—Aiming and firing instruction.
2½ hours.—Extended order drill.
2 hours.—Squad drill.
1 hour.—Physical training.

SATURDAY.

2 hours.—Squad drill.
1 hour.—Bayonet fighting.
1 hour.—Physical training.

## 5th Week.

MONDAY.

3 hours.—Route march to training area. Extended order drill.
1 hour.—Squad drill
1 hour.—Bayonet fighting.
1 hour.—Physical training.
2 hours.—Musketry. Tests of elementary training.

TUESDAY.

2 hours.—Musketry. Tests of elementary training.
4 hours.—Squad drill and guards. Posting and relieving sentries.
1 hour.—Lecture on interior economy.
1 hour.—Physical training.

WEDNESDAY.

3 hours.—Route march to training area. Judging distance.
1 hour.—Squad drill.
1 hour.—Bayonet fighting.
1 hour.—Physical training.
2 hours.—Musketry. Miniature range shooting, grouping and application.

THURSDAY.

2 hours.—Musketry. Snap shooting.
3 hours.—Squad drill and guards.
2 hours.—Extended order.
1 hour.—Physical training.

FRIDAY.

3 hours.—Route marching to training area. Visual training.
1 hour.—Extended order.
1 hour.—Musketry.
1 hour.—Collective practices.
1 hour.—Physical training.
2 hours.—Elementary night training. 8.15—10.15 p.m. drill and visual training.

SATURDAY.

2 hours.—Musketry instruction. Go over the work done during the week.
1 hour.—Lecture on discipline.
1 hour.—Physical training.

---

## ADVANCED TRAINING AT BLANDFORD.

On arrival at Blandford officers and men will be formed into platoons and drafted into the reserve battalions, which will consist of companies graded in efficiency; the fresh formed platoons joining the bottom company of the ladder and gradually the entire company works it way to the top and becomes the draft finding company. Having sent off its draft the company staff return to the bottom rung and repeat the process.

The course at Blandford is to last seven weeks, the 1st—3rd weeks consisting of guard duties,* fitting equipment, platoon training and recruits' course of musketry.

The 4th—6th weeks are to be devoted to company training.

The 7th week to classification and field firing practices.

Syllabus A. and B. are a guide as to what points chief attention should be paid.

## SYLLABUS "A."

*Suggested Course of Platoon Training.*

The following elementary lessons should be taught by means of lectures and demonstrations, and repeated until each man has pigeon-holed the lessons in his head.

This form of training is only suitable for platoons to begin with :—

1. March discipline.
2. Lines of small columns.
3. Extended order.
4. Rushes.
5. Reorganisation of sections.
6. Passing messages.
7. Use of ground and cover.
8. The assault on a trench in four lines. The first two lines carrying rifles and bayonets, the third line carrying dummy bombs, hand grenades and shovels. The fourth line carrying sandbags.
9. Rapidity of loading, aiming and firing at heads and shoulders on open ground and from constructed trenches.
10. Fire direction and fire control. Practice in trenches.
11. Visual training and judging distance.
12. Covering fire. Demonstration from trenches.
13. Teaching men to go over obstacles, by means of planks and ladders.
14. Elementary night training in the following progressive stages :—
    - (*a*) Platoon drill in the dark.
    - (*b*) Movements by whispered words of command.
    - (*c*) Putting on and taking off equipment in the dark.
    - (*d*) Handling entrenching tools in the dark.
    - (*e*) Occupying entrenchments and relieving troops already in trenches. Two sections relieving the other two sections.
    - (*f*) Visual training in the dark and training sentries for outpost work.

---

* Guard duties are to be kept as low as possible.

15. Handling of a piquet on outpost duty.
16. Instruction to leading seamen and men in group duties.
17. Conduct of reconnoitring patrols in the field.
18. The action of a rear party in a rear guard.
19. Field fortifications :—
    (*a*) Use of material in the field, such as sandbags, stones, hurdles, brushwood, timber and wire netting.
    (*b*) The handling of a working party by day and by night.
    (*c*) Excavation of trenches. Use of entrenching implements.
    (*d*) Construction of head cover and loopholes.
    (*e*) Method of making shelter trenches.
    (*f*) Construction of obstacles, high and low wire entanglements.
    (*g*) Use of hand grenades and bombs in trenches.
    (*h*) Revetting existing entrenchments.
20. Bayonet fighting and mess tin cooking in the field.

Any attempt to teach large units these lessons will result in the majority of the men receiving no instruction whatever.

## SYLLABUS "B."

*Company Training.*

The following tactical exercises should be carried out during the fourth, fifth and sixth weeks :—

1. March out from camp to suitable ground and carry out at least three days a week the following lessons already carried out in platoon training :—

    Lessons Nos. 1, 2, 3, 4, 5, 6, 8, 10, 11, and 12.

    In lessons 1 to 12 the Company Commander should carefully note how Platoon and Section Commanders handle their commands.
2. The handling of a company as an advanced guard to a battalion—
    (*a*) Encountering small hostile patrols.
    (*b*) Encountering enemy when O.C. main body wishes to attack.
    (*c*) Advanced guard taking up a defensive position.

N.B.—Company Commanders should make Platoon and Section Commanders write field messages during this work, learn to read a map and interpret written instructions forwarded from Company Commanders during the day's operations. All Platoon Commanders on return to camp should write a report on the day's operations.

3. The defence of a village by a company forming part of a battalion :—

(*a*) Delaying defence } by day and night.
(*b*) Active defence }

The following villages, when held, bring out excellent lessons and are very instructive to all ranks :—

(1) Tarrant Monkton.
(2) Tarrant Hinton.
(3) Pimperne.
(4) Tarrant Rushton.
(5) Tarrant Keynston.

4.—(*a*) Company in trenches carrying out an assault on a line of trenches about 100 to 200 yards away, shovels, sandbags and bombs to be used (day and night).

(*b*) Company in reserve in shelter trenches carrying out an assault over the fire trenches, crossing by miniature bridges (day and night).

5. Company on outpost duty to a battalion entrenched.
6. The defence of a river line.
7. Company taking up a billeting area.
8. Rear guard to a force retreating.
9. The attack and defence of a wood (forming part of a battalion).
10. The attack on a village.
11. Bivouacs—company should be absent from camp over night.

---

www.ingramcontent.com/pod-product-compliance
Ingram Content Group UK Ltd.
Pitfield, Milton Keynes, MK11 3LW, UK
UKHW040020200726
13854UKWH00001B/283

9 781845 741617